CONFLICT RESOLUTION
In Search of Peace

Tuhin K Das

Conflict Resolution: In Search of Peace
Tuhin K Das

Independently published, December 08, 2018

ISBN: 9781790959280

CONTENTS

PREFACE

Google search would give you a vast list of books on conflict, conflict management and conflict resolution. Then why there is another book? I must not claim it an exclusive book but it is different from others. It is based on a theory developed very recently - Conflict Resolution Curve Theory or CRC model. This book contains its derivation and application in various conflict situations whether it is interpersonal or interstate or terrorism. This model is very simple to apply based on some uncomplicated computations. Moreover, gravity of the problem can be well understood diagrammatically.

I hope this book will be useful to students and researchers of social studies, political science and defence studies. I am grateful to my family for their cooperation and patience during the time of writing this book.

Tuhin K Das
December 08, 2018

World experienced in past and is experiencing till now myriad of conflicts starting from ethnic conflicts to cold war. However, society always talks about peace though the path from conflict to peace is not well defined. It varies from place to place, community to community and time to time and everyone justifies their own paths. It has been observed that most countries use violence to solve disputes. Even some Buddhist nations have been engaged in conflicts and they justify their violence as a defense and for the sake of peace.[1] Here the question arises how to resolve conflict. Is it in a violent or a non-violent way? People are clearly in a dilemma. The present book has been aimed at solving this problem by using a simple model. This model has been applied in three specific cases: interpersonal conflict, interstate conflict, and also conflict between terrorists and Institution. Applications reveal some interesting outcomes which are realistic too.

Conflict Management vs. Conflict Resolution

Generally two approaches are aimed to traverse the path from conflict to peace: conflict management and conflict resolution. In literature, conflict management and conflict resolution are often used synonymously. But some differences between these two nomenclatures do exist. In a website posted by the Human Resources of Iowa State University *"managing conflict implies that the conflict exists, but it is controlled in such a way that the conflict is not a major problem. On the other hand, resolving conflict means that some end or solution to the conflict has been determined."* [2]

According to Elleni Bereded-Samuel, *"conflict management involves taking action to keep a conflict from escalating further (which) implies the ability to control the intensity of a conflict and its effects through negotiation, intervention, institutional mechanisms and other traditional methods. (While) Conflict resolution, generally, seeks to resolve the incompatibilities of interests and behaviours that constitute the conflict by recognizing and addressing the underlying issues, finding a mutually acceptable process and establishing relatively harmonious relationships and outcomes."* [3]

In another study, the distinction has been made as follows: *"conflict management is a pro-active method* in preventing conflicts by…. (Whereas) conflict resolution involves techniques used after the occurrence of a conflict." [4]

Swanström and Weissmann concluded that "*conflict management and conflict resolution are different concepts, but at the same time they are closely interrelated. They are two mechanisms at different sides of a continuum, used to deal with the same conflicts but at different stages of these conflicts.*" [5] They further added that "*the process of conflict management is the foundation for more effective conflict resolution. A distinction between conflict management and conflict resolution is, however, needed as a starting point as the concepts often are confused or integrated in an inappropriate manner. Conflict resolution refers to the resolution of the underlying incompatibilities in a conflict and mutual acceptance of each party's existence, while conflict management refers to measure that limit, mitigate and/or contain a conflict without necessarily solving it.*"

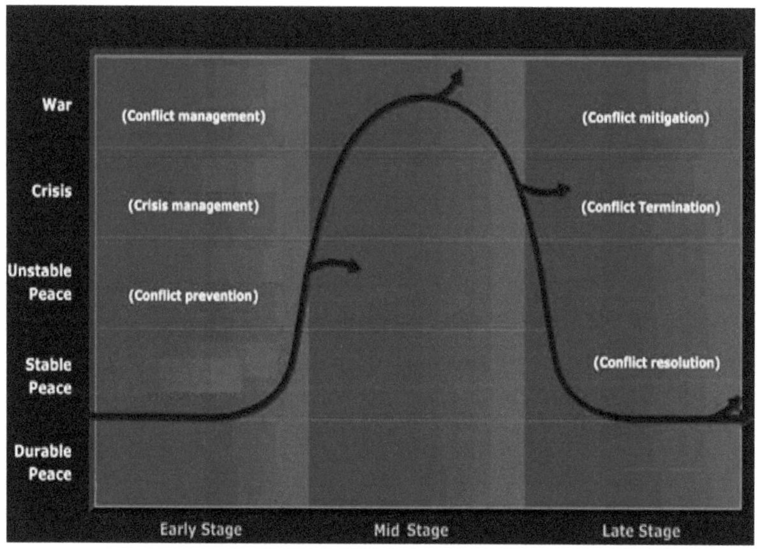

Fig. 1.1: Curve of conflict (Lund Curve)*

So, in a nutshell, **conflict management** is mainly engaged in controlling the intensity of a conflict and its impacts through various institutional mechanisms whereas **conflict resolution** is involved in identifying, addressing and finding mutually acceptable solutions of the underlying issues of conflict. But in reality these two processes cannot be clearly distinguished. They are somehow mixed up during the course of conflict. For example, **Lund curve** (also called **curve of conflict**) describes the course of a conflict along with various phases of

---

* Source: United States Institute of Peace Negotiation and Conflict Management Notice
https://communicationwithoutborders.wordpress.com/2012/11/10/negotiation-and-conflict-management/

peace-building actions as it rises and falls in intensity over time (Figure 1.1).

Michael Lund derived this curve in relation to two dimensions - the intensity of conflict and the duration of conflict.[6] It helps in imagining the evolution of conflict. According to this curve, effort to mitigate conflict when there is an outbreak of violence may be termed as conflict management. It happens in the mid-stage of conflict. Conflict resolution (or settlement) happens in the last stage of conflict. During the unstable and crisis periods in the early stage of conflict he termed the peace-building strategies as conflict prevention and crisis management.

So, the very idea of conflict resolution as described above is somehow mixed up with other strategies in the curve of conflict. Bifurcation of policies into management and resolution may happen at any point of time in early stage or mid-stage or last stage of conflict. It is not always a sequential decision process. A hypothetical model is illustrated in the next chapter based on human behaviour that exemplifies that bifurcation of policies is possible at any point of time depending on mutual understanding. The model reveals that some changes in parametric values might cause bifurcation of policies

in controlling conflict that might lead to ultimate
peace.

Lord Krishna's teachings to Arjuna on war and non-violence[†]

[†] Source: Jeffery D Long (October 2009), War and Non-violence in the
Bhagavad-Gita, https://www.esamskriti.com/e/Spirituality/Bhagavad-
Gita/War-And-Non-Violence-In-The-Bhagavadgita-1.aspx

CHAPTER 2
CONFLICT RESOLUTION THEORY

Conflict resolution modelling needs clear understanding of causes of conflict and its resolution which are very complex. There are various dimensions (or attributes) in any conflict situation. Different authors tried to identify those attributes. For example, power, temperament, culture, context, relationship, values, experiences, etc. influence the outcome (or style) of a conflict.[7] Different values (generally qualitative) of these attributes cause different conflict styles. Conflict style is a condition to meet one's needs in a conflict (or dispute) but may impact other people in different ways. For example, conflicting parties using **accommodating** style *"yield their needs to those of others, trying to be diplomatic. They tend to allow the needs of the group to overwhelm their own, which may not ever be stated, as preserving the relationship is seen as most important."* [8]

A simple conflict resolution model in this context is Dual Concern Model. The underlying theory proposes five types of conflict styles based on two dimensions: assertiveness (concern for self) and empathy (concern for others). Conflict style changes depending on the weightage assigned to each dimension. In literature, conflict styles have been named differently but they have the same significance. Generally, they are characterised as (Figure 2.1):

- ➢ **Competition**: Higher weightage on assertiveness and lower weightage on empathy
- ➢ **Accommodation**: Lower weightage on assertiveness and higher weightage on empathy
- ➢ **Collaboration**: Higher weightages on both assertiveness and weightage on empathy
- ➢ **Avoidance**: Lower weightages on both assertiveness and empathy
- ➢ **Compromise**: Moderate weightages on both assertiveness and empathy

Dual concern model has been statistically tested and observed that variance of conflict styles could be explained mostly by the above two dimensions (Sorenson et al. 1999).[9] But the importance of motivation has been felt, especially, in explaining conflict styles like "collaboration" and "compromise". Understanding its importance, a theoretical model is presented here where motivation (self or by third party) is an intrinsic part. Regret analysis has been used as a tool to formulate this model.

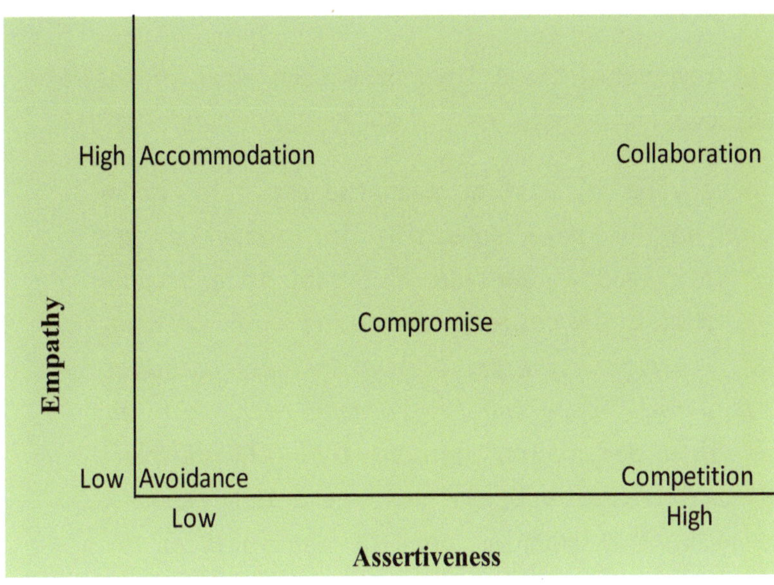

Fig. 2.1: Dual Concern Model

Definitions

Here are some definitions that have been used in the proposed model:

Cost: Generally, by cost we mean the amount of money needed to buy or make something in production and delivery of a good or service. But cost in a broader sense includes *monetary valuation of effort, material, resources, time and utilities consumed, risks incurred, opportunity forgone etc. in any action.*[10] This definition implies that all monetary expenses are costs, but all costs are not expenses such as risk. For example, cost of war includes not only the prices of arms and ammunition, wages of army, etc. but also risks of injury, life-loss, loss of sovereignty and so on.

Regret: According to Cambridge Dictionary, regret means one's feeling of sadness about a situation, especially something sad or wrong or a mistake that he/she has made. But in decision theory, *regret is defined as the experience or anticipation of sadness or disappointment which is caused by making a wrong choice (when there are other options open to them).* People take this experience/anticipation into consideration when making decisions.[11]

Probability: (Objective) Probability is the chance that something will happen. But can we measure such an abstract notion? In reality, what we achieve is the *subjective probability.* It is *"derived from an individual's personal judgment about whether a specific outcome is likely to occur. It contains no formal calculations and only reflects the subject's opinions and past experience."* [12] In that sense, subjective probability always differs from person to person, and contains a high degree of personal bias.

Cost Matrix: A cost matrix is a tool that is used to simplify all of the possible outcomes (in terms of cost) of a strategic decision. Let A and B are two conflicting entities (individuals or groups or countries). A's decision has two dimensions: assertiveness (concern for self) and empathy (concern for others). Conflict style changes depending on the weightage or importance given to each dimension. Suppose various weightages on "concern for others" be alternative decisions of A, say less (low) and more (high) (Table 2.1). Suppose A has no concern for B if B is aggressive. On the other hand, A has concern for B if B is non-aggressive. Now the outcome of the decision taken by A varies depending on the actions taken for "concern for self". Suppose C_{ij} is the cost associated with i^{th} concern for self and j^{th} concern for B (i.e., j^{th} action of B). This cost may include damage cost due to conflict and cost of self-defence (viz., legal advice, arm force, weapons, etc.).

Table 2.1: Cost Matrix

	Less concern for opponent (B)	More concern for opponent (B)
	B is aggressive with Probability P	B is non-aggressive with Probability (1-P)
Less concern for self (A)	C_{11}	C_{12}
More concern for self (A)	C_{21}	C_{22}

Regret Analysis

In the above cost matrix, regret felt by A for the decision "less concern for other" when B is non-aggressive is the additional cost for deciding "more concern for self".[13] It is:

(2.1) $R_1 = C_{21} - C_{11}$

Similarly, the regret felt by A for the decision of "more concern for other" when B is aggressive is the additional cost for deciding "less concern for self". It is:

(2.2) $R_2 = C_{12} - C_{22}.$

Suppose P is the probability of B to be aggressive and (1-P) is the probability of B to be non-aggressive. This probability is difficult to estimate. Nevertheless, A assumes that there is some (high/moderate/low) chance of threat from B. So, what is assumed by B is the subjective probability when the objective probability is P (say). Similarly, C_{ij} is difficult to measure. In spite of this difficulty, A imputes some value to it. On the basis of these imputed costs and subjective probability, the expected cost when A is less concerned for self is

(2.3) $L_1 = P\ C_{11} + (1-P)\ C_{12}$

Similarly, the expected cost when A is more concerned for self is

(2.4) $L_2 = P\,C_{21} + (1-P)\,C_{22}$

To an unconcerned entity: $L_1 = L_2$, which after simplification reduces to:

(2.5) $R_2/R_1 = P/(1-P)$

Equation (2.5) is rewritten as

(2.6) $RR = f(P)$

Where $RR = R_2/R_1$ and $f(P) = P/(1-P)$, a function of P.

Interpretation of the Result

At this point, it is highly needed to interpret RR and $f(P)$ otherwise this result would become irrelevant. Regret is an emotional state. However, there is a judicial sense of regret.[14] Some aspects of regret do not necessarily involve emotion but cognitive processes of memory, judgment or evaluation. So,

Proposition 1: From A's point of view R_2 is a function of judgement of B's badness and R_1 is a function of judgement of B's goodness. The ratio RR $(= R_2/R_1)$ signifies the comparison of badness and goodness of B as judged by A. Value of RR $<$ 1 indicates that A is more inclined to peace-building than violence, and RR $>$ 1 signals A's more inclination to violence than to submission or negotiation. RR = 1 signifies his/her apathy towards violence.

The function f(P) is a ratio of two parameters, probability of aggression and probability of non-aggression. It was observed that the probability of aggression is a linear function of judgments of badness of opponent, i.e., A.[15] Then (1−P) may be assumed to be a function of judgments of goodness of A. Therefore,

Proposition 2: f(P) reveals the comparison of badness and goodness of *A* as judged by *B*. Value of f(P) increases as *A* is judged to be more bad than good, and decreases as *A* is judged to be more good than bad. So, for a good *A* as judged by *B*, peaceful solution of conflict is expected. [16]

Conflict Resolution Curve

The function f(P) is drawn against P in Figure 2.2. Following Propositions 1 and 2, it may be argued that *A'*s comparison of badness and goodness of *B* coincides with *B'*s comparison of badness and goodness of *A* on this curve.

This curve shows that the value of f(P) increases as P increases.

R_2/R_1 = f(P) > 1 if P > ½ . It implies that R_2> R_1. Thus *A* would feel more regret for the decision of "more concern for *B*".

On the contrary, R_2/R_1 = f(P) < 1 if P < ½. It implies that R_1> R_2. It means that *A* would feel more regret for the decision of "less concern for *B*".

In the above equation, RR = 1 if P = ½, i.e. R_1 = R_2. So, for an unconcerned one, regrets R_1 and R_2 are equal provided others are not much aggressive (P = ½). This is a compromising solution in dual concern model.

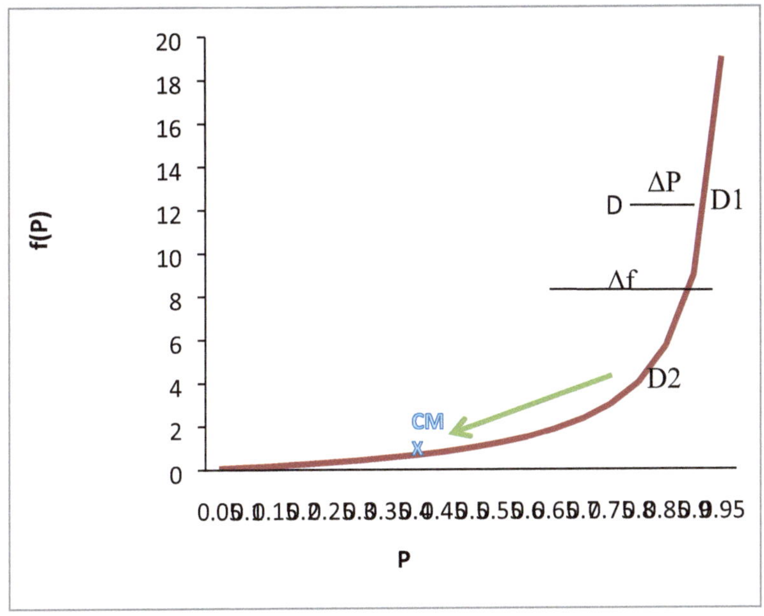

Fig. 2.2: Conflict resolution curve

It is possible to reach the compromising solution CM (corresponding to P = ½) along this curve by reducing R_2, i.e., by reducing probability of aggressiveness P. Ultimately, peace can be achieved by reducing P further, i.e., by increasing R_1. Henceforth, this curve has been called *conflict resolution curve* (CRC). [17]

Let us now consider other conflict styles of dual concern model. In the case of "dominance/competition", $L_1 > L_2$, which after simplification reduces to

(2.7) $RR > f(P)$

Inequality (2.7) represents the region above the "conflict resolution curve". Let D be a point in this region. It represents the conflict style "dominance/competition" of *A*. Now the question is how could *A* shift from conflict style "dominance/competition" to conflict style "compromise"? This type of conflict resolution could be accomplished firstly by moving from point D to some points in conflict resolution curve. There are two ways to achieve it:

Approach-1: move to point D_1 by increasing probability of aggressiveness by ΔP keeping f(P) constant, or

Approach-2: move to point D_2 by decreasing functional value f(P) by Δf keeping P constant.

Approach-1 implies more aggressiveness of *B*, say by increasing militarisation. In this case, *A* is bound to reduce the ratio R_2/R_1 provided *A* is weaker than *B*. This is possible when costs associated with "more concern for self", i.e., C_{21} and C_{22} increase (Table 2.2). This is a very common method observed throughout the world, forcing A to come to negotiation table.

Approach-2 is a different method where motivation plays an important role by not intensifying aggressiveness. Decrease of f(P) in relation (2.6) implies decrease of RR, i.e., increase of R_1 with respect to R_2 or decrease of R_2 with respect to R_1. This can be achieved by decreasing costs C_{11} and C_{12} (Table 2.2). One way to do this is motivating *A* to "concern less for self" (say, by some assurance from *B* or third party). Examples of such conflict resolution are observed in some regions. [18]

Table 2: Motivation ($\uparrow$ indicates increase; $\downarrow$ indicates decrease)

Strategy	C_{11}	C_{12}	C_{21}	C_{22}	R_1	R_2	RR
Approach-1			$\uparrow$			$\uparrow$	$\downarrow$
Approach-1				$\uparrow$	$\downarrow$		$\downarrow$
Approach-2	$\downarrow$				$\uparrow$		$\downarrow$
Approach-2		$\downarrow$				$\downarrow$	$\downarrow$

The conflict resolution point D_2 is better than the point D_1 because of less aggressiveness of B (i.e., lower value of P) and its closeness to compromising solution CM. Forcing an entity to compromise might invoke another conflict.

Finally, peace can be achieved by reducing P more and more after reaching the conflict resolution curve. It implies reduction of R_2 as far as possible. The applicability of this hypothetical model is tested in Chapters 3–5.

Singularity of CRC

Let us assume that RR $<$ f(P) for some value of P, say, the point M (blue triangle) in Figure 2.3. It implies that the *A* judges *B* better than what the *B* actually is. Ideally *A* should be at point E since *B* is at that point corresponding to that value of P. This situation is similar to *accommodating style* of conflict in Dual Concern Model.

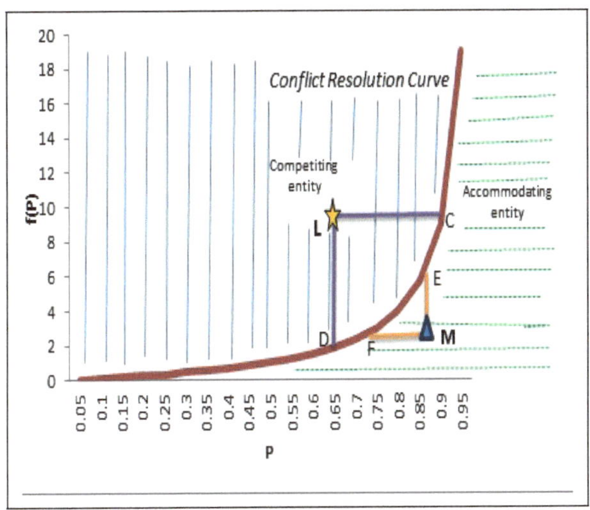

Fig. 2.3: Negotiable points on CRC

It is understood from the above discussion that the conflict resolution curve separates conflict styles into two separate domains: domain of competing entities and domain of accommodating entities. There is a sort of agreement between targets and aggressors on this curve. Their judgements of badness compared to goodness of each other are analogous on this curve. So, arrival of all conflicting entities to some negotiable points on CRC is important before peace building. Does this emerge in reality?

Conflicting situation as at point M in Figure 2.3 appears in non-violent movement. At point M the judgement of B (suppressor of non-violent movement) is worse than that of A (social actors involved in non-violent movement). So, B tries to suppress such movements shifting the conflict situation to point E. But in recent decades nonviolent struggles ultimately toppled repressive regimes from power and sometimes forced leaders to change the nature of governance, i.e., shifting to point F. [19]

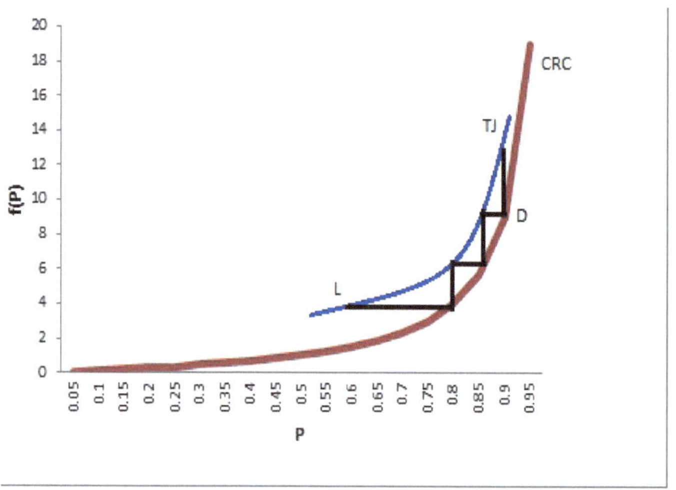

Fig. 2.4: Dynamics of conflict resolution by competing entities

Examples of competing entities are multifarious starting from inter-state conflict to intra-state conflict. In the case of competing entities, B might enhance their chance of aggression from position L to the point C and compelling A to resolve conflict. But it is also possible that A might increase RR by increasing R_2 (the regret experienced by the target due to the decision of "more concern for B" when B is more aggressive) or decreasing R_1 (the regret experienced by A because of the decision "less concern for B" when B is less non-aggressive). Afterwards, B might boost aggression to a higher level. This is a non-ending conflicting situation represented by the zigzag black lines in Figure 2.4. Blue line in Figure 2.4 illustrates the path of A' s judgement (TJ) of B' s attitude over time. Both the curves CRC (red line) and TJ (blue line) move towards each other (not necessarily converging) as the conflict continues. Generally, at some point of time entities both B and A agree to resolve conflict by shifting the conflicting situation to point D in Figures 2.3 and 2.4. It suggests lessening of P of B and RR (i.e., R_2) of the target. Recent development in Korean Peninsula is such an example.[20]

The function f(P) is singular at P=1. Thus CRC does not exist in reality if the chance of aggression of B is hundred per cent (at least from the computational point of view). Is it possible to explain this outcome in the light of Omnipotent Mathematics?[21]

The function $f(P) = 1/0$ at P=1. The outcome of such a numerical expression would be in quasi-existence according to Omnipotent Mathematics (OM). A quasi-existent outcome is a state in between existence and non-existence. For example, $0 = i + (-i)$ and $i \times (-i) = 1$, where $i = \sqrt{-1}$. Here 0 is a non-existent entity, i and $(-i)$ are quasi-existent entities and 1 is an existent entity. By some mathematical operations defined in OM, it can be shown that $1/0 = q$ or $-q$, where q and $-q$ are quasi-existent entities.

Let us now try to interpret quasi-existent outcome in the context of CRC? It might be an outcome involving destruction or damage on a catastrophic scale. The state of Germany after World War-II was not non-existent outcome (not complete destruction of Germany) but quasi-existent outcome (only fall of Nazi Germany and country's division in two parts). The German reunification in 1990 is the transition process from quasi-existence to existence.

At the point of singularity (i.e., P=1) of the function $f(P)$, the RR (ratio of regrets) of A might also become singular. If A feels no regret for the decision "less concern for the aggressor", then $R_1=0$ and RR=1/0. It obviously leads to apocalypse with mutual destruction. Fortunately, human society has not experienced such a situation where P=1 (i.e., chance of aggression of B is hundred per cent) and $R_1=0$ (i.e., A has no regret for not concerning for B) simultaneously.

CHAPTER 3
INTERPERSONAL CONFLICT

Interpersonal conflict is a reality of life and can occur anywhere, from working place to personal relationships. For instance, there is a wide range of interpersonal conflicts or disputes among neighbours or residents within a community though types of such conflicts are different. Conflict of interest is a major type among them. Causes of such conflicts are disagreement over distribution of money, space, common facilities, etc. *Resolving it as early as possible is important for everyone because situations are not so entrenched and others are less likely to have started to take sides and the negative attitudes are not so extreme. The best way to address a conflict in its early stages is through negotiation between the participants.* [22]

A typical interpersonal conflict is discussed here for better understanding of conflict resolution process discussed in the previous chapter. In an Apartment House consisting of eight apartments, the water distribution system is shown in Figure 3.1. Overhead water reservoirs for each apartment are shown by the numerals in the corresponding boxes. Chamber 9 is allotted to common use like cleaning of garage spaces, roof, community-hall, etc. It is larger than other chambers 1-8 (nearly 1½ times of the volume of other chambers). Source of water is the Municipality-Water-Supply and lifted to overhead tank by Lift-Pump. There was an agreement among apartment owners not to disturb this distribution system individually.

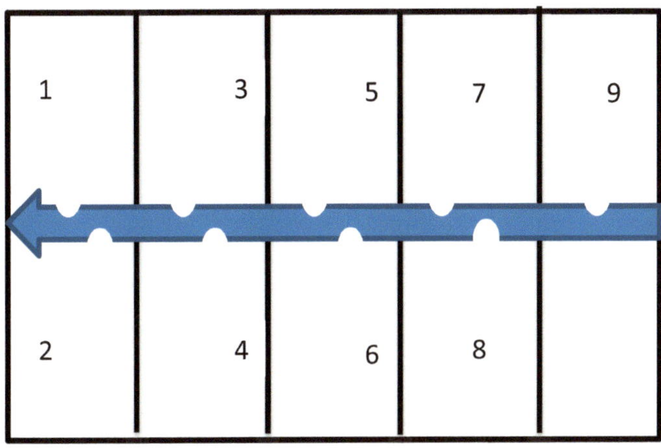

Fig. 3.1: Layout of the overhead tank

But one Apartment-owner (say, Apartment-1) was unhappy with this system. Due to lack of maintenance of the distribution-pipe (thick blue arrow line), water distribution was not uniform in all Chambers. Water supply reduces as it moves from Chamber-9 to Chambers-1 and 2. So, one fine morning he started using the water of Chamber-9 by an unauthorised connection. Result was a conflict between that

Apartment-owner and the rest. The cost matrix for
this problem is calculated on the basis of equivalent
annual cost (EAC) of different cost components as
follows:

A. Cost incurred by Apartment-1 for unauthorised water
   connection = 1237
B. Additional cost for disconnection when others were
   aggressive = 356
C. Getting less water (Cost of water from other sources) =
   1400
D. Getting more water due to others cooperation for
   redistribution of water = 700
E. Contribution towards maintenance of water system = 100

Then C_{ij}'s are computed as:

a. C_{11} =   C
b. C_{21} =A+B
c. C_{12} =C+E
d. C_{22} =C-D+E

The resulting cost matrix (Table 3.1) is

Table 3: Cost Matrix for Apartment-1

	Less concern for other	More concern for other
	Aggressive with Probability P	Non-aggressive with Probability (1-P)
Less concern for self	1400	1500
More concern for self	1593	800

Then his regret for the decision "less concern for others" when others are non-aggressive is R_1 = 193, and his regret for the decision of "more concern for others" when others are aggressive is R_2 = 700, i.e., RR = R_2/R_1 = 3.63. Probability of others being aggressive corresponding to this value is 0.78. But he estimated from his previous experience the probability of others being aggressive as 0.60 (i,e., nearly in 60 per cent of cases others acted aggressively against his previous actions).

Point D (denoted by star mark) in Figure 3.2 shows his position at that time (with probability = 0.60 and RR = 3.63). There were two options to other Apartment owners: either (1) to persuade him to bring to point O_1 or (2) to compel him to move to point O_2. Second option means "more aggressiveness" of others.

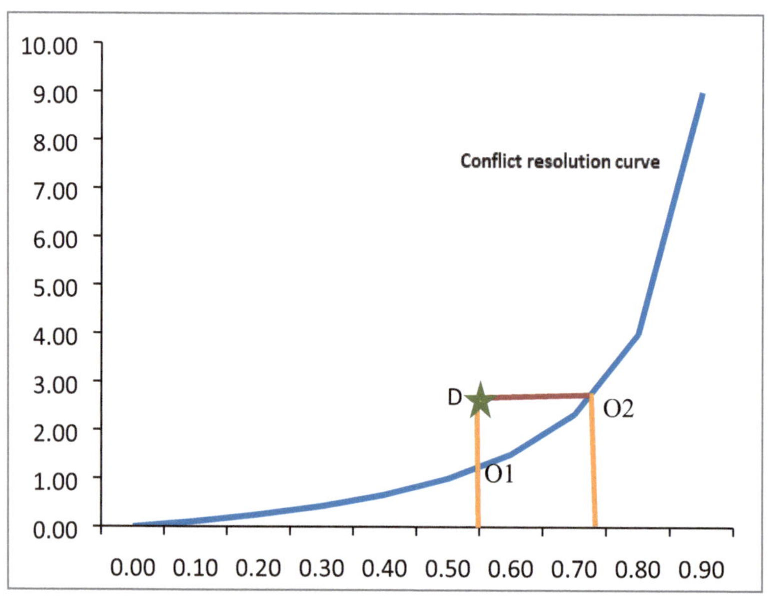

Fig. 3.2: Options for conflict resolution (P1 and P2)

In this case Option-2 did not work. More aggressiveness aggravated the conflict among them even in other common programs. Therefore, other Apartment-owners tried Option-1, i.e., to motivate him to disconnect the new water connection under certain condition. Conditions are proper maintenance of distribution pipe, monitoring of water supply so that everyone gets same volume of water, etc. The negotiation is still under process.

CHAPTER 4
INTERSTATE CONFLICT

World enjoyed the period of "long peace" since the end of WW-II in 1945.[23] This period witnessed no direct war between major powers in spite of the risk of conflicts (viz., during the period of Cold War). The concept of "long peace" remains highly controversial. Scholars have argued that "long peace" is not uncommon in history[24], but it may be temporary.[25] Various reasons have restrained the leaderships of the major powers from international war for more than 70 years. Reasons were the threat of mutual destruction by nuclear arsenal, disastrous experience of last two World Wars, anti-war democratic voices, and globalisation.[26] But recent global unemployment crisis[27], protectionist policy[28] and terrorism[29] pose new threats to international peace.

There is a saying: a small spark can start a great fire. During the long peace period there was no great war. But who knows that a relatively smaller interstate conflict or foreign military intervention in intrastate conflicts might emerge as a major international war due to some ignored or apparently insignificant reasons. At present there are number of military conflicts or flexing of muscles throughout the world. Examples are interstate conflicts between North Korea and USA, Russia and Ukraine, Israel and Palestine, India and Pakistan, China and both the Philippines and Vietnam in the South China Sea; and also intrastate conflicts with foreign military intervention like civil war in Syria and war against IS in Iraq. [30]

Thousands of articles have been published so far elaborating what conflict might trigger WW-III. Some of these articles are amazing to read. North Korea has been blamed mostly by the international community for the coming nuclear war. Is it so easy to forecast the future apocalypse? Let us analyse the North Korea crisis in the light of conflict resolution curve and find the feasibility of any such war. [31]

Cost Matrix of North Korea

Cost matrix (Table 4.1) for an individual is somehow easy to compute. But such computation is difficult for a nation in interstate conflict as it is not known whose interests play in conflict and negotiation process. Always there remain some hidden costs that are not mentioned explicitly. Here we compute two cost matrices considering the (a) interests of nation and (b) interests of ruler.

The cost matrix corresponding to the interests of the Nation is calculated on the basis of annual cost of different cost components as follows:

A. GDP of North Korea (Source: https://www.cnbc.com/2017/07/20/less-than-one-aircraft-carrier-the-cost-of-north-koreas-nukes.html)
B. Decline in GDP (say, 15 per cent of GDP)
C. North Korea's total defence spending per year (Source: https://www.lovemoney.com/gallerylist/68382/americas-defence-budget-versus-north-koreas)
D. Cost of internal security (say, 10 per cent of defence spending)
E. Expected loss in GDP growth (say, 2.5% of GDP) due to paying more concern for others

Then C_{ij}' s are computed as:

a. C_{11} = B (Negative impact on economy due to aggression of opponents)
b. C_{21} =C (Defense spending)

c. C_{12} =E (Sacrifice)

d. C_{22} =0 (Negligible militarisation)

The resulting cost matrix (Table 4.1) is

Table 4.1: Cost Matrix of the Nation (Billion USD)

	Less concern for other	More concern for other
	Others are aggressive with probability P	Others are non-aggressive with probability (1-P)
Less concern for self	6	1
More concern for self	10	0

The Nation's regret for the decision "less concern for others" when others are non-aggressive is $R_1 = 4$, and its regret for the decision of "more concern for others" when others are aggressive is $R_2 = 1$, i.e. RR = R_2/R_1 = 0.25. Probability of others being aggressive corresponding to this value is 0.2.

So, the nation should be near the conflict resolution curve. A slightest increase in the probability of aggressiveness of the opponents would transform it to either accommodating or compromising entity. But we observed a different scenario. North Korea did not stop its nuclear tests and missile launching in spite of imposing a series of sanctions by United Nations.[32]

United States and its allies demonstrated a show of force by conducting repeated military exercises over and near the Korean Peninsula. It implies that P, the probability of aggressiveness of opponents was high. Why did this happen? To find the solution we compute the cost matrix corresponding to the interests of the Ruler.

Computation is based on country's spending on luxury goods as follows:[33]

F. Estimated spending on luxury goods (Source:
    http://time.com/8651/north-koreas-kim-spending-big-on-
    cars-cognac-pianos/) + correction by simulated values
G. North Korea's total defense spending per year (Source:
    https://www.lovemoney.com/gallerylist/68382/americas-
    defence-budget-versus-north-koreas)
H. Cost of internal security (say, 10 per cent of defense
    spending)

Then C_{ij}'s are computed as:

e. C_{11} = F (Removed from power)
f. C_{21} = G (Defense spending)
g. C_{12} = F (Sacrifice)
h. C_{22} = G (Defense spending after denuclearisation, say,
    10%)

The resulting cost matrix (Table 4.2) is:

Table 4.2: Cost Matrix of the Nation (Billion USD)

	Less concern for other	More concern for other
	Others are aggressive with probability P	Others are non-aggressive with probability (1-P)
Less concern for self	6.5	6.5
More concern for self	10	1

The result is presented in Table 4.2. The Ruler's
regret for the decision "less concern for others"

when others are non-aggressive is $R_1 = 3.5$, and its regret for the decision of "more concern for others" when others are aggressive is $R_2 = 5.5$, i.e., RR = R_2/R_1 = 1.57. Probability of others being aggressive corresponding to this value is 0.61. It should be mentioned here that the above calculation is based on an earlier estimate of F. It may be much higher at present time. So, the predicted P would be higher than the computed value. If we consider 2 per cent annual growth in spending on luxury items by the Ruler and associates, then P would come to about 0.72.

The above result justifies why the Ruler of North Korea now agrees to denuclearisation after escalating the threat to high value by opponents. It was required to raise the value of P to nearly 0.61 (or more taking into consideration the correction) to transform the style of conflict from competing to compromise. Actually we have no idea how the Ruler of North Korea values the (subjective) probability of aggressiveness of United States and its allies. It may be higher because his unexpected move in recent times shows that he is willing to change the conflict style from competition to compromise.

CHAPTER 5
CONFLICT BETWEEN TERRORISTS AND INSTITUTION

There is no universally agreed definition of terrorism. *Different bodies, organisations and government agencies have different definitions to suit their own particular role, purpose or bias.*[34] The Federal Bureau of Investigation in United States of America describes terrorism as *the unlawful use of force and violence against persons or property to intimidate or coerce a government, the civilian population, or any segment thereof, in furtherance of political or social objectives.*[35] The Terrorism Act 2000 in UK defines terrorism as *the use or threat of action designed to influence the government or an international governmental organisation or to intimidate the public, or a section of the public; made for the purposes of advancing a political, religious, racial or ideological cause; and it involves or causes serious violence against a person or serious damage to a property or a threat to a person's life or a serious risk to the health and safety of the public or serious interference with or disruption to an electronic system.* Thus there no unique definition and it is always difficult to get a universally accepted database of terrorism though the acts of terrorism have increased markedly in recent decades.

However, Global Terrorism Database (GTD) has been generated using the following definition: "*The threatened or actual use of illegal force and violence by a non-state actor to attain a political, economic, religious, or social goal through fear, coercion, or intimidation.*" [36]

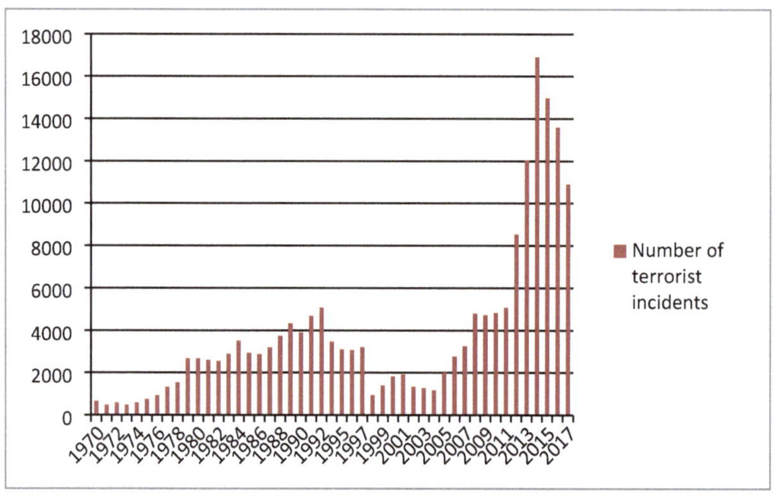

Fig. 5.1: Number of terrorist incidents in the world
(Source: GDT 2018)

According to this database a trend in terrorism in the world can be obtained over the period 1970-2017 (Figure 5.1). The trend shows that there was a decline in terrorist incidents in late 1990s and early 2000s. But at that time the terrorist incidents were becoming incredibly deadly. [37]

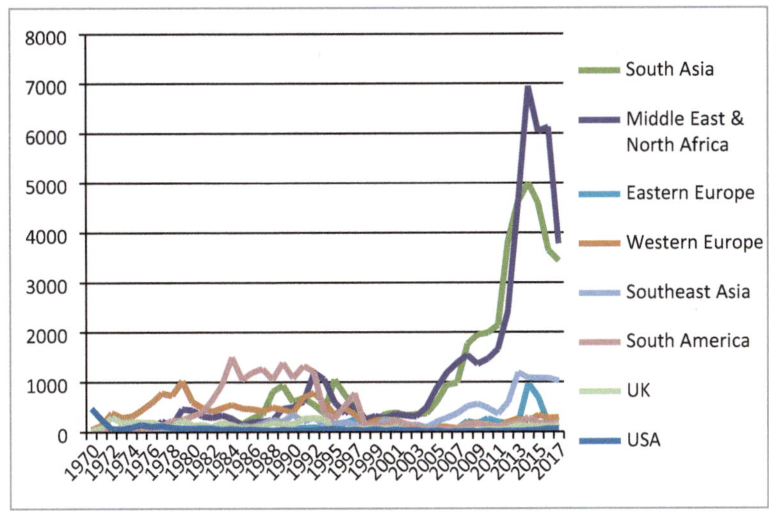

Fig. 5.2: Region-wise Number of terrorist incidents
(Source: GDT 2018)

Terrorism suddenly increases in the present decade even in developed nations; although the main contributors are Asian countries. So, terrorism is a major headache of the day – be it Islamic or ultra-leftist or ethnic. Now the question is: Is the brutal force against terrorists is the only way to challenge terrorism? The present analysis is an attempt to answer the above question in terms of a two-party conflict: Terrorists and the Institution.[38] But the real difficulty in solving such a problem is that there is often a third party who wages a shadow war against the Institution by providing money and logistics to terrorists.[39] It implies that terrorists' activities in any country are motivated by others who indirectly involve in the confrontation. In this regard, conflict resolution curve theory might be applied to find peace-building path in conflicts that are aggravated by third party interference. Conflict resolution curve theory incorporates motivation - in bad or good sense - through a cost matrix to evaluate regret of two parties involved in conflict resolution.

Cost Matrix

As we described in Chapter 2, let A and B are two conflicting parties (say, terrorist/antagoniser and the Institution/target). A's decision has two dimensions: assertiveness (concern for self) and empathy (concern for others). Conflict style changes depending on the weightage or importance given to each dimension. Terrorists' activities intensify by giving low weightage to empathy (i.e., no concern or less concern for others). If A gives no weightage to assertiveness and at the same time does not keep any concern for others, then he/she is not supposed to respond to any motivation. Religion, ethno-regionalism, etc. are major motivators of terrorism. But other motivations also act. It has been observed that families of suicide bombers receive large sums of money, social status and reputation after the attack.[40] Since A does not experience any gain or loss in terrorist activities because of apathy towards religion or ethno-regionalism, he/she remains unresponsive to motivators. Thus cost C_{11} in Table 5.1 should be zero.

Giving higher weightage to assertiveness while keeping low concern for others indicate more organised terrorist activities like launching sabotage or suicide attacks which require well-trained sophisticated terrorist groups.[41] In this conflict style, there are chances of being caught or killed and the expected cost of risk (death or punishment) is much higher than previous one. But training and sophistication of such attacks need money. Moreover, there are risks of injury, death, captivity and sentences. These factors cause higher cost of C_{21} than C_{11} in Table 5.1.

Table 5.1: Cost matrix

	Aggressiveness of Institution with probability P	Non-aggressiveness of Institution with probability (1-P)
Concerns	Low concern for others	High concern for others (Exit strategy for terrorists pretending to be concerned for others)
Low concern for self	C_{11} *(Unresponsive to motivators, i.e., no loss or no gain)*	C_{12} *(Submission with a risk of threat from left out terrorist group)*
High concern for self	C_{21} *(Responsive to motivators which*	C_{22} *(Terrorists' gain through negotiation)*

	involve higher cost of training, arms and risk of life)	

New situation arises when economic, social and personal rewards from third party are withdrawn. On the contrary, the Institution offers packages for giving up terrorism. In Table 5.1, this situation has been described as terrorists' concern for others. But sometimes the story is different. Terrorists search for an exit strategy when the cost of risk surpasses benefits from third party. Under such circumstances they often pretend to be concerned for others. Anyway, two conflict styles emerge here:

1. *Submission* which implies faith in Institution and giving lower importance to self-interest (viz., interest in terrorism ideology that was counselled by motivators). Generally, youths who had joined the cult of terrorism started to realise their mistakes and they wish to get back into the mainstream.[42] But it is very difficult and dangerous to leave the terrorist group. The security of the willing terrorist as well as that of his/her family comes under threat from the same group. So, the cost C_{12} might be very high.

2. *Negotiation* which implies faith in Institution giving at the same time higher importance to self-interest. The associated cost C_{22} in Table 5.1 may

be negative as terrorists generally gain through negotiation.[43] Generally, this peace-building strategy is asymmetrical and costlier for Institutions than it is for terrorists. On the other hand, non-negotiation means aggravated violence and sometimes negotiations can be an exit strategy for terrorists who have second thoughts about their struggles.

Regret Analysis

Terrorists may experience regret by taking a decision for any particular action when there are other ways to act. Various weightages on "concern for others" are alternative decisions of terrorists. Let R_1 be the regret experienced by a terrorist because of the decision "less concern for Institution" when the Institution is non-aggressive. It could be measured by the additional cost of deciding "more concern for self". Similarly, R_2 is the regret experienced by a terrorist due to the decision of "more concern for Institution" when the Institution is aggressive. In the same way, it could be measured by the additional cost of deciding "less concern for self". Here

$$R_1 = C_{21} - C_{11} \text{ and } R_2 = C_{12} - C_{22}.$$

$R_2 > 0$, since C_{12} is always higher than C_{22} (negotiation fetches more benefits than submission). Similarly, $R_1 > 0$, since C_{21} is always greater than C_{11}

(C_{21} includes cost of risk of injury, death, captivity, etc. and cost of training and weapons).

As it has been discussed earlier, there is a judicial sense of regret. Some aspects of regret do not necessarily involve emotion but cognitive processes of memory, judgment or evaluation. So, from terrorists' point of view R_2 is a function of judgement of the Institution's badness and R_1 is a function of judgement of the Institution's goodness. The ratio RR:

$$RR = R_2/R_1 > 0$$

This result signifies the comparison of badness and goodness of the Institution as judged by a terrorist. Value of RR < 1 indicates that the terrorist is more inclined to peace-building than terrorism and RR > 1 signals terrorists' more inclination to terrorism than to submission or negotiation. RR = 1 signifies their apathy towards terrorism.

Conflict resolution curve theory deduces that for an unconcerned person, assuming P as the aggression of *B*,

$$RR = f(P) \text{ where } f(P) = P/(1-P)$$

The function $f(P)$ is a ratio of two parameters, probability of aggression and probability of non-aggression. It was observed that the probability of aggression is a linear function of judgments of badness of opponent, i.e., terrorist. Then (1-P) may be assumed to be a function of judgments of goodness of terrorist. Therefore, f(P) reveals the comparison of badness and goodness of terrorists as judged by the Institution. Value of f(P) increases as a terrorist is judged to be more bad than good, and decreases as he/she is judged to be more good than bad. So, for a good terrorist as judged by the Institution, peaceful solution of conflict is expected.

Following Propositions 1 and 2 in Chapter 2, it may be argued that Terrorists' comparison of badness and goodness of the Institution coincides with the Institution's comparison of badness and goodness of terrorists on Conflict Resolution Curve (CRC). The value of the function f(P) reduces with decreasing value of P. It means that at any point with lower value of P, the Institution and terrorists judge each other more "good" than "bad", than that at any other point with higher value of P. So, a leftward movement along this curve is an approach to peace building.

Actually, P is the subjective probability of the Institution's aggression and P is the objective probability of the Institution's aggression. But it is assessed as P from terrorists' personal judgment, i.e., P is a subjective probability. P is assessed by terrorists on the basis of the actions taken by the Institution or terrorists' perception about the Institution after they are brainwashed by motivators. It contains no formal calculations and only reflects terrorists' opinions and past experiences.

An interesting situation arises during conflict. There might be two possible happenings: either $P > \bar{P}$ or $P < \bar{P}$. Figure 5.3 represents the case where $P > \bar{P}$. The blue line in the figure is the CRC. Terrorist's position (point T) lies above this curve. But the Institution (point S) with objective probability of aggression $\bar{P}$ lies below the position of terrorist. Here the Institution has to take the decision whether (i) it would increase $\bar{P}$ up to the point R by acting in more aggressive way (i.e., fighting) or (ii) convince the terrorist to give up aggression and bring him/her to point S (i.e., compromise).

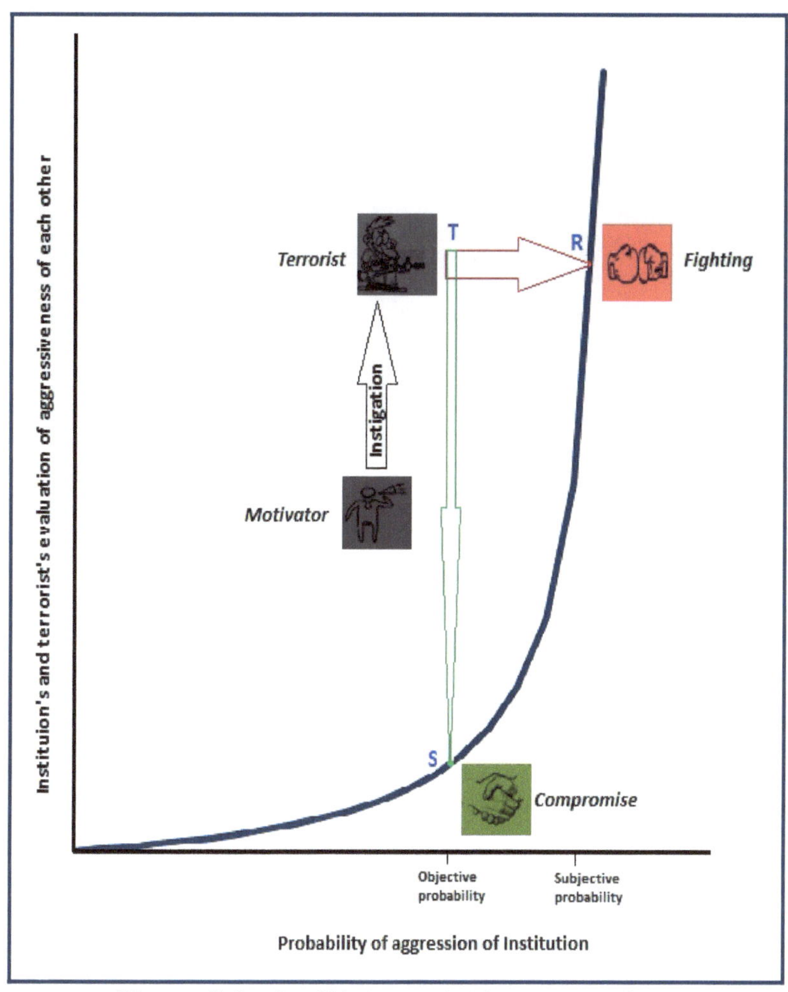

Figure 5.3: Conflict resolution strategies

Decision (2) does not usually work. It has been discussed earlier that terrorists' activities are generally influenced by motivators. Motivators' instigation (black upward arrow) play as push factors in terrorism. It may be verified by reducing the cost

C_{21} in the cost matrix. This really happens when motivators provide financial and logistic supports to terrorists. Lower value of C_{21} decreases the value of R_1, which in turn increases the value of RR. Thus acts of motivators work against the good gesture of the Institution (green downward arrow). The only solution in this case is to (a) delink the terrorists from motivators and/or (b) neutralize motivators.

CHAPTER 6
WHAT WE HAVE ACHIEVED

There are many examples of conflict resolution in history, and there has been a debate about the means to conflict resolution: whether it should be forced or peaceful. Conflict resolution by peaceful means is always a better option. The conflict resolution curve derived in Chapter 2 suggests two options: aggressive action and non-aggressive effort. Sometimes non-aggressive efforts lead to conflict resolution. Forced resolution of conflict by non-aggressive effort might invoke another conflict in future. [‡] It was observed that Government policy of recognition of more languages of the diverse population of northeast states in India reduces conflict. [44]

The applicability of the CRC model has been tested in Chapter 3. The case study is about an interpersonal conflict situation. The case study unveils that conflict resolution by motivation is a better option than conflict resolution by force. It is an on-going negotiation process and it is hoped that some peaceful solution might come out.

[‡] (https://www.ushmm.org/wlc/en/ article.php?ModuleId=10007428)

Next the CRC model has been applied in an interstate conflict situation. Application shows that the interest of the ruler rather than the interest of the nation plays the decisive role to predict styles of conflict in Korean peninsula. Results of the model also indicate how the present crisis might be solved towards peace building. The on-going negotiation process in North Korea might verify how far this model is applicable in reality.

Third application of model is in the case of terrorism. In conflict resolution, malicious motivator is always a challenge. Such motivators work as push factor in terrorism. Their negative roles cannot be ignored in terrorism. So, attempt to confront only terrorists without any actions on malicious motivators is not the effective way to resolve conflict between terrorists and the Institution. Here their interference has been examined by using a cost matrix and it has been inferred that actions against the motivators are necessary for real peace building.

Thus what we have achieved in Conflict Resolution Curve Theory is its applicability in various conflict situations whether it is interpersonal or interstate or terrorism. It is very simple to apply based on some uncomplicated computations. Moreover, gravity of the problem can be well understood diagrammatically.

REFERENCES

1 Shadbolt, Peter, Conflict in Buddhism: 'Violence for the
  sake of peace?' (April 23 2013),
  https://edition.cnn.com/2013/04/22/world/asia/buddhism-
  violence/index.html
2 Conflict Management or Conflict Resolution? (accessed
  November 30, 2018),
  https://www.extension.iastate.edu/hr/conflict-
  management-or-conflict-resolution
3 Bereded-Samuel, Elleni (September 2006), Conflict
  Resolution versus conflict Management, The Conflict
  Resolution Conference: Resolving External Community
  Conflict, Melbourne,
  www.ourcommunity.com.au/files/kms/Elleni_%20Bereded_%20S
  amuel.ppt
4 Jan Leentvaar, Conflict Analysis: Management and
  Resolution (accessed November 30 2018), UNESCO-IHE,
  http://www.ais.unwater.org/ais/pluginfile.php/79/course/
  section/127/Microsoft%20PowerPoint%20-
  %203%20Conflict%20resolution.pdf
5 Swanström, Niklas L.P. and Mikael S. Weissmann (2005),
  Conflict, Conflict Prevention, Conflict Management and
  Beyond: A conceptual exploration, CONCEPT PAPER,
  https://www.files.ethz.ch/isn/113660/2005_swanstrom-
  weissman_concept-paper_conflict-prevention-management-
  and-beyond.pdf
6 United States Institute of Peace(January 30 2008),
  Certificate Course in Conflict Analysis,
  https://www.usip.org/sites/default/files/academy/OnlineC
  ourses/Conflict_Analysis_1-30-08.pdf
7 Curtis, John (November 21 2012), The 8 Factors that
  Influence How You Handle Conflict,
  https://www.johncurtis.ca/conflict-resolution/the-8-
  factors-that-influence-how-you-handle-conflict/

[8] Office of Human Resource Development, University of Wisconsin-Madison (2017), Conflict Styles, https://www.talent.wisc.edu/home/HideATab/LeadershipManagementDevelopment/ConflictResolution/AboutConflict/ConflictStyles/tabid/228/Default.aspx

[9] Sorenson, R. L., E. A. Morse and G. T. Savage (1999), A Test of the Motivations Underlying Choice of Conflict Strategies in the Dual - Concern Model, International Journal of Conflict Management, Vol. 10, Issue 1, https://www.researchgate.net/publication/235320513_A_Test_of_the_Motivations_Underlying_Choice_of_Conflict_Strategies_in_the_Dual-Concern_Model

[10] Business Dictionary, http://www.businessdictionary.com/definition/cost.html

[11] Regret Theory Definition, INVESTOPEDIA, https://www.investopedia.com/terms/r/regrettheory.asp

[12] Subjective Probability, https://www.investopedia.com/terms/s/subjective_probability.asp

[13] Das Tuhin K (May 4, 2018), Regret Analysis towards Conflict Resolution, SSRN Electronic Journal, (Available at SSRN: https://ssrn.com/abstract=3173490 or http://dx.doi.org/10.2139/ssrn.3173490)

[14] Landman, Janet (1987), Regret: A Theoretical and Conceptual Analysis, Journal for the Theory of Social Behaviour, 17 (2), https://deepblue.lib.umich.edu/bitstream/handle/2027.42/73569/j.1468-5914.1987.tb00092.x.pdf?sequence=1&isAllowed=y

[15] Hynan, Michael T. and Judith A. Esselman (1981), Victims and aggression, Bulletin of the Psychonomic Society, Vol. 18 (4), 169-172, https://link.springer.com/content/pdf/10.3758/BF03333594.pdf

[16] Zunes, Stephen (2009), The Power of Nonviolent Action,

eJournal USA, Volume 14 (3),
https://kr.usembassy.gov/wp-content/uploads/sites/75/2017/04/Nonviolentej.pdf

[17] Das, Tuhin K. (June 15, 2018), Conflict Resolution Curve: Concept and Reality, Available at SSRN: https://ssrn.com/abstract=3196791

[18] Das, T. K., I. Das Gupta, S. K. Haldar and S. Mitra (2015), Conflicts and Socioeconomic Consequences in Northeast India, Asian Journal of Humanities and Social Studies, Volume 3, Issue 1, pp. 79-84

[19] Zunes, Stephen (2009), The Power of Nonviolent Action, eJournal USA, Volume 14 (3), https://kr.usembassy.gov/wp-content/uploads/sites/75/2017/04/Nonviolentej.pdf

[20] Davenport, Kelsey (June 2018), Chronology of U.S. - North Korean Nuclear and Missile Diplomacy, Published on Arms Control Association, https://www.armscontrol.org/factsheets/dprkchron

[21] Das, Tuhin K (June 2015). Omnipotent Mathematics to Explain Singularity, Researchgate, https://www.researchgate.net/publication/279200599_Omnipotent_Mathematics_to_Explain_Singularity

[22] An Introduction to Conflict Resolution (accessed December 06, 2018), https://www.skillsyouneed.com/ips/conflict-resolution.html

[23] Gaddis, John Lewis (Spring, 1986), The Long Peace: Elements of Stability in the Postwar International System, International Security, Vol. 10, No. 4, pp. 99-142

[24] Siverson, Randolph M. and Michael D. Ward (Summer, 2002), The Long Peace: A Reconsideration, International Organization, Volume 56, Issue 3, pp. 679-691, https://doi.org/10.1162/002081802760199926

[25] Clauset, Aaron (2017), The Enduring Threat of a Large

Interstate War, An OEF Research Discussion Paper,
http://dx.doi.org/10.18289/OEF.2017.018

[26] Price, Michael (February 21, 2018), Are We in the Middle
of A Long Peace—or on the Brink of A Major War?,
Science, http://www.sciencemag.org/news/2018/02/are-we-
middle-long-peace-or-brink-major-war

[27] UN News (January 22, 2018), Unemployment to remain high,
quality jobs harder to find in 2018 - UN labour agency,
Economic Development,
https://news.un.org/en/story/2018/01/1000901

[28] Kirk, Ashley (November 28, 2017), Mapped: Protectionism
is on the Rise as US And EU Implement Thousands of
Restrictive Trade Measures, The Telegraph - Business,
https://www.telegraph.co.uk/business/2017/11/28/mapped-
protectionism-rise-us-eu-implement-thousands-
restrictive/

[29] Guéhenno, Jean-Marie (August 9, 2017), From Al-Qaida to
ISIS, A Blind War on Terrorism Will Mean Endless War,
World Politics Review,
https://www.worldpoliticsreview.com/articles/22910/from-
al-qaida-to-isis-a-blind-war-on-terrorism-will-mean-
endless-war

[30] Global Conflict Tracker (2018), Center for Preventive
Action, https://www.cfr.org/interactives/global-
conflict-tracker#!/global-conflict-tracker

[31] Das, Tuhin K. and Datta Ray, Ishita (June 10, 2018),
North Korea's Peace Building in the Light of Conflict
Resolution Curve, SSRN Electronic Journal,
https://ssrn.com/abstract=3193759 or
http://dx.doi.org/10.2139/ssrn.3193759

[32] Westcott, Ben and Joyce Tseng (September 15, 2017),
Timeline: North Korea nuclear tests versus United
Nations sanctions, CNN,
https://edition.cnn.com/2017/01/20/asia/north-korea-
nuclear-sanctions-timeline/index.html

33 Rauhala, Emily (February 19, 2014), North Korea's Kim
Spending Big on Cars, Cognac, Pianos, Time,
http://time.com/8651/north-koreas-kim-spending-big-on-
cars-cognac-pianos/
34 Gregor Bruce (May 2013), Definition of Terrorism: Social
and Political Effects, Journal of Military and
Veterans' Health, Volume 21, Number 2,
https://jmvh.org/wp-content/uploads/2013/06/Definition-
of-Terrorism.pdf
35 John Philip Jenkins (October 26, 2018), Terrorism,
Encyclopaedia Britannica,
https://www.britannica.com/topic/terrorism
36 Max Roser, Mohamed Nagdy and Hannah Ritchie (2018),
Terrorism, Our World in Data,
https://ourworldindata.org/terrorism
37 The Guardian (April 17, 2013), Four decades of US terror
attacks listed and detailed,
https://www.theguardian.com/news/datablog/2013/apr/17/fo
ur-decades-us-terror-attacks-listed-since-1970
38 Das, Tuhin K. (November 14, 2018), Confronting
Terrorism: A Hypothetical Approach, SSRN Electronic
Journal, https://ssrn.com/abstract=3284310 or
http://dx.doi.org/10.2139/ssrn.3284310
39 Bruneau, Emile (November 2016), Understanding the
Terrorist Mind, Cerebrum, cer-13-16,
https://www.ncbi.nlm.nih.gov/pmc/articles/PMC5198759/
40 Bruce, Gregor (August 2013), Intrinsic and External
Factors and Influences on the Motivation of Suicide
Attackers, Journal of Military and Veterans' Health,
Volume 21 Number 3, https://jmvh.org/wp-
content/uploads/2013/09/Gregor-Bruce-from-
JMVH_August_2013-5.pdf
41 Gronlund, Lisbeth, David Lochbaum and Edwin Lyman
(December 2007), Nuclear Power in a Warming World, Union
of Concerned Scientist,

https://www.ucsusa.org/sites/default/files/legacy/assets/documents/nuclear_power/nuclear-power-in-a-warming-world.pdf

[42] Singh, Jaibans (September 2017), Surrender is the Best Recourse for Local Terrorists in J&K, Indian Defence Review,
http://www.indiandefencereview.com/news/surrender-is-the-best-recourse-for-local-terrorists-in-jk/

[43] Brandt, Patrick T., Justin George and Todd Sandler (September 2016), Why Concessions should not be Made to Terrorist Kidnappers, European Journal of Political Economy, Volume 44,
https://www.sciencedirect.com/science/article/pii/S0176268016300143

[44] Das, Tuhin K., Ivy Das Gupta, Sushil K. Haldar and Sudakhina Mitra (February 2015), Conflicts and Socioeconomic Consequences in Northeast India, Asian Journal of Humanities and Social Studies, Volume 03, Issue 01

9 781790 959280